THIS
B♡♡K
BEL♡NGS
T♡ ♡

# Color Your World with Creativity and Self-Love

In a world that often feels overwhelming, nurturing our minds and hearts is more important than ever. The journey we've been on has tested us, but through it all, we've learned the power of self-care. By embracing creativity, we open the door to joy and inner peace, filling our lives with color and light. Let art be your guide to healing, your source of strength, and a reminder that even in the toughest times, we have the abiliity to create happiness from within.

## Keeping it Affordable: Tips for a Better Coloring Experience

We've chosen this paper with affordability in mind, aiming to provide a great product at a reasonable price. For the best results when using pens or markers, we suggest placing a thicker sheet behind the page to avoid any bleed-through. We truly appreciate your understanding and want you to know this decision was made with your experience in mind!

Blank sheet of paper

Babe Carpenter

# COLOR TEST PAGE

SWAN
SERENADE

Thank you from the bottom of my heart for purchasing this coloring book. Your support means the world to me, and I am truly honored that you've chosen to bring my creations into your life.

Every book I create is made with you in mind, inspired by the hope of bringing a little joy, creativity, and relaxation to your days. Whether you're unwinding after a long day, sharing moments with loved ones, or simply indulging in some "you" time, I hope this book becomes a source of happiness and peace.

It's your support and enthusiasm that fuels my passion to keep creating. Please know that with each page you color, you're not just adding beauty to the world but also inspiring me to continue this journey.

Thank you for allowing me to be part of your creative moments. I can't wait to bring you more books to enjoy!

With heartfelt gratitude,


Babe Carpenter

Made in the USA
Coppell, TX
28 January 2025